Chip Carving the Southwest

with Pam Gresham

Text written with
and photography by
Douglas Congdon-Martin

Schiffer Publishing Ltd

77 Lower Valley Road, Atglen, PA 19310

DEDICATION

I dedicate this book to my husband Peter. His devotion to woodcarving and woodworking keeps me always inspired. He is a true craftsman.

ACKNOWLEDGMENTS

I would like to thank my family and friends for helping me so much through each of my endeavors.

I would also like to extend my sincere appreciation to Douglas Congdon-Martin, Peter and Nancy Schiffer, and all the wonderful people at Schiffer Publishing. It is a special place with special people!

Copyright 1994 by Pam Gresham
Library of Congress Number: 94-66373

Printed in the United States of America
ISBN: 0-88740-699-8

Published by Schiffer Publishing, Ltd.
77 Lower Valley Road
Atglen, PA 19310
Please write for a free catalog.
This book may be purchased from the publisher.
Please include $2.95 postage.
Try your bookstore first.

We are interested in hearing from authors
with book ideas on related subjects.

Preface

This book is the first of a number of topical books on chip carving. Chip carving lends itself to so many wonderful designs. When people think of chip carving, the traditional European designs generally come to mind. In this book I use traditional chip carving techniques to create Southwest designs. Because they are geometric in form, Southwest motifs lend themselves to chip carving.

I see chip carving evolving into new designs, but it evolves by integrating designs of various historical cultures with designs that enjoy popularity today. Our society is a mesh of many diverse cultures. Our art reflects that mesh, no matter what the medium. The technique of chip carving lends itself so beautifully to the expression of traditional art of different backgrounds. Yet mixing the traditional with a little unusual adds new excitement to any art form. Even chip carving!

My first book, *Basic Chip Carving with Pam Gresham,* gave an extensive explanation of each cut. This book, *Chip Carving the Southwest,* takes for granted that the reader has some knowledge of the techniques required to chip carve.

Included in this book is a pattern for each piece pictured, and the layout process required to make the pattern fit the size or shape of the readers' piece. In addition, complete carving instructions for the plate pictured on the cover and the candle box with the eagle on the front are included. The reader can carve the pieces that do not include carving instructions by drawing from the instructions given for the plate and candle box. The designs have many similarities.

I believe this to be a useful chip carving book. I hope my experience and instructions save you frustration. I want to give each chip carver the ability to create wonderful pieces.

Contents

Introduction

The dominant tribes that make up the native Americans of the Southwest are the Apache, Pueblo and Navajo. Through their artwork and crafts I gathered and adapted these designs for chip carving. I researched the sand paintings, weavings, pottery, baskets, jewelry, clothing, accessories, and ceremonial items of these tribes and their sub tribes. Through research, I tried to insure that these patterns truly represent the designs of the Southwestern Indians.

Some symbols have significance to these Indian tribes. According to *Indians of the Western States*, published by Dexter Press, Inc., the Thunderbird is the sacred bearer of happiness unlimited. Crossed arrows mean friendship. The design used on the fireplace match holder is an adaptation of a butterfly design that stands for everlasting life. A single arrow means protection and the zig-zag border resembles a mountain range. Eagle feathers mean Chief.

I find myself always looking for the meanings behind designs, no matter what culture I am researching. In each instance I find disagreements between people relating to the existence and meanings in certain designs. I mean to offend no one with my interpretations. I enjoy, as I believe many people do, knowing part of the history behind the motif I am carving. The artwork becomes a conversation piece with a sense of history and meaning to it. I find this intriguing.

I began to carve Southwest motifs when I redecorated our home in Southwest decor. The designs I created surprised and pleased me. My husband, who is a much better painter than I, painted them with Southwest colors. These patterns quickly became some of my favorites to carve. They are fun designs. Precision is always striven for in chip carving, but is not such a necessity when carving these patterns.

In this book I concentrate on chip carving. I do not discuss specific woodworking details. I feel there are numerous woodworking books, magazines, and shows that deal with that subject. The limited space within this book needs to deal with aspects of chip carving. I do give measurements for some pieces, and I hope that is sufficient for most woodworkers. These designs can and should be adapted to your pieces.

You may need to size the drawings for your piece on a copy machine by either enlarging or reducing the pattern. Do not be afraid to mix and match the designs. Change the borders and combine different patterns. There are numerous possibilities contained within this book.

Remember to select and prepare your wood carefully before putting the pattern onto the piece. I recommend basswood for chip carving. Remember the rule, the whiter and lighter the wood, the easier carving it will prove to be. The large thunderbird plaque is butternut. It is a good carving wood, not as grainy feeling to the knife as it appears with the eye. Notice that I chose a large, relatively simple design for this wood. A geometric either tends to get lost in the grain or appears too busy. I painted this design to make it stand out from the grain.

Be sure to sand your piece thoroughly before putting the pattern onto it. Always sand with the grain. Some gentle hand sanding may be required after carving, but only to remove any stubborn pencil marks. Be careful not to sand over any sharp edges because this dulls them and takes the crisp, clean look from the carving. Pieces also tend to break out easily at this point.

Since the publication of my first book, many people have called and asked me what I use to finish my pieces. I have to be honest with them as I do with you here. My husband, Peter, is also a professional carver. He was professional long before I was. He carves in-the-round and relief carvings. He developed the stain we use now for his carvings. Pete spent many hours mixing different chemicals, applying the mixtures to small pieces of basswood, then numbering and timing each. From these experiments, and years of trial and error, he developed beautiful stains. There are no commercial products that compare in color quality and do not blotch on basswood. My point in telling this to you, the reader, is that I promised my husband before writing *Basic Chip Carving* that I would not tell the staining mixtures and processes we use. We still make our living by selling our carved products. We feel that our stains and finishes are part of what sets our work apart from the work of other carvers. There has been such a positive response to our stains that we are looking into selling them to the public. I cannot say for sure at this point.

If you need a recommendation, after some trial and error with the stains presently on the market, I recommend that you try the Carver Tripp stains. Two shows on the Public Broadcasting network, "This Old House" and the "New Yankee Workshop" also recommend these stains. These are water based stains that come in several colors and do not tend to blotch on basswood. Carver Tripp also makes a water based polyurethane that I believe might work for you. Please accept my honesty and sincerity on this matter. My intentions are to write the best books on design and techniques for chip carvers. Finishing techniques could be another complete book. There are several books dealing with that subject.

For those of you not familiar with my first book, *Basic Chip Carving with Pam Gresham*, it is a detailed book on the tools and techniques of chip carving. Included in that book is a detailed tool list for drawing and carving, discussions of knife sharpening techniques, knife positions, how to select and prepare the wood, and basic geometric concepts. It explains at length the technique used to execute each type of cut used in chip carving. The book examines chip carving from the easiest to the hardest cuts. If you need a detailed description of any of the following cuts please refer to that book. This Southwestern book is a natural progression from the original book.

Good luck, and I hope you enjoy carving these patterns as much as I do!

The tools for chip carving are simple. They involve several measuring and layout tools, pencils, erasers, and, of course, knives.

The basic knife positions will require some practice to perfect. Throughout the book we refer to Position 1 and Position 2. This is Position 1. You grasp the handle firmly with the blade facing you. The middle joint of your index finger should be where the back of the blade meets the handle. Keep the hand completely on the wood. The placement of the thumb is the tricky part, and the hardest to endure while learning. It is necessary to learn this correctly because it will keep you from slicing your thumb.

The inside joint of the thumb should be at the very end of the wooden handle. The blade of the knife will almost be on your thumb. Bend the thumb slightly backward at the middle joint, and place the tip of the thumb on the board. The thumb and the knife will always move together as you cut.

Occasionally you will use a stab knife to create decorative cut. This knife does no cutting. You grasp the knife firmly with the beveled edge of the blade toward you. Press down firmly at the point where the cut begins...

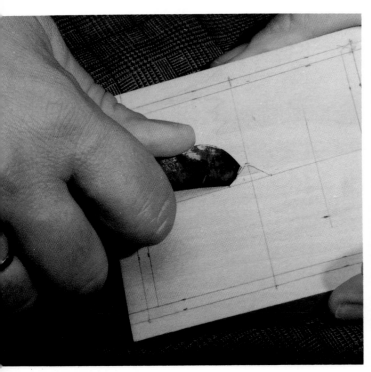

In Position 2 the knife is held with the blade facing away from you. The thumb is on the back of the knife with a little tip of the thumb (1/2") on the back of the blade. Wrap the rest of you fingers around the knife handle. The cut is away from the body.

and rock the knife back toward you. Return the knife to vertical and take it out. With these three basic knife techniques almost all of chip carving can be done.

Patterns

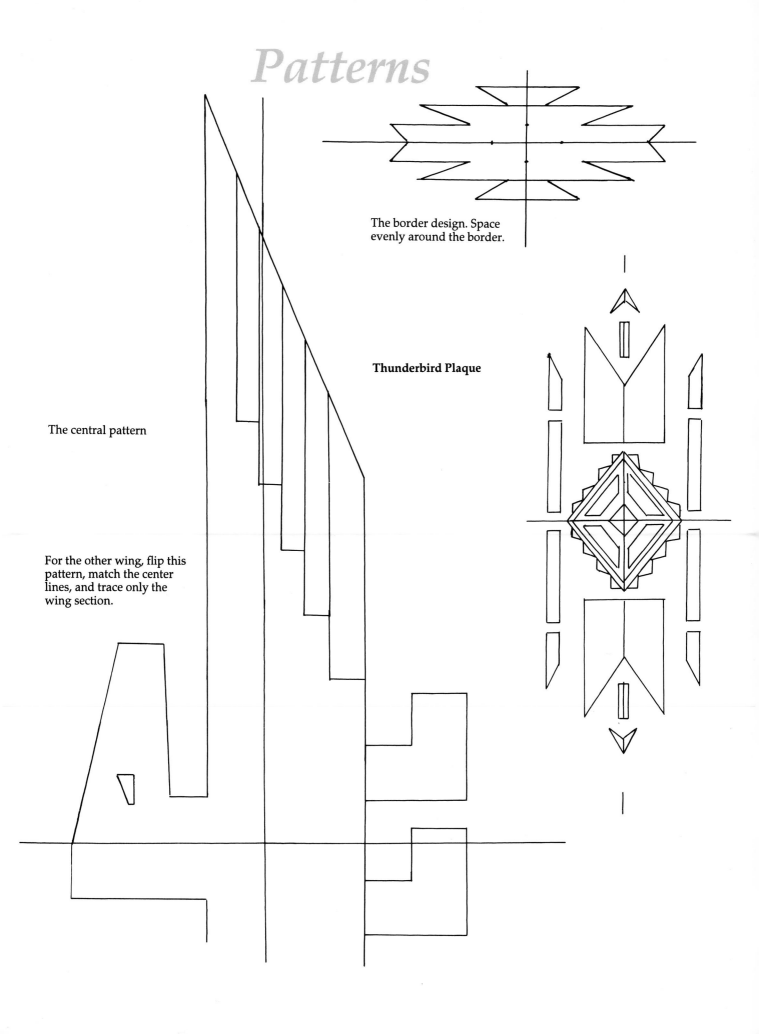

The border design. Space
evenly around the border.

Thunderbird Plaque

The central pattern

For the other wing, flip this
pattern, match the center
lines, and trace only the
wing section.

Southwest Plate Patterns

Central pattern. Flip the
design to trace the other
side.

Rim pattern.

Pattern for fireplace
matchholder, kitchen
utensil or dried flower
holder.

8

Border of the framed plate.
Here too there are marks
for setting the compass.

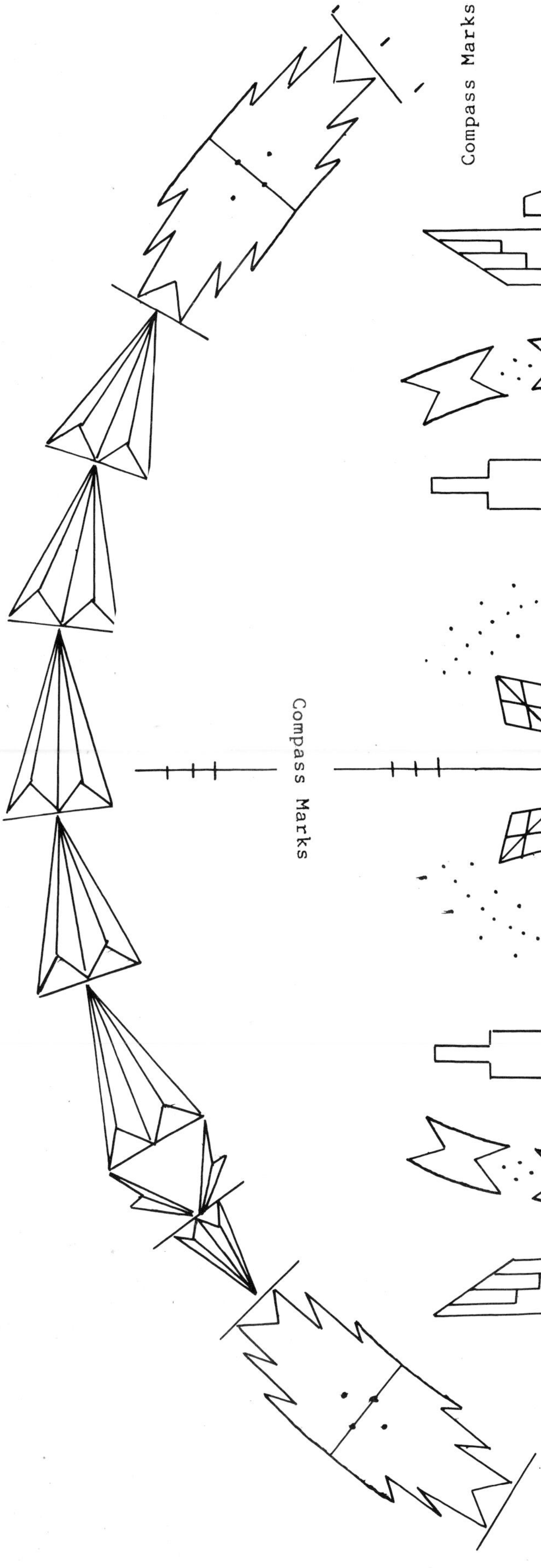

Compass Marks

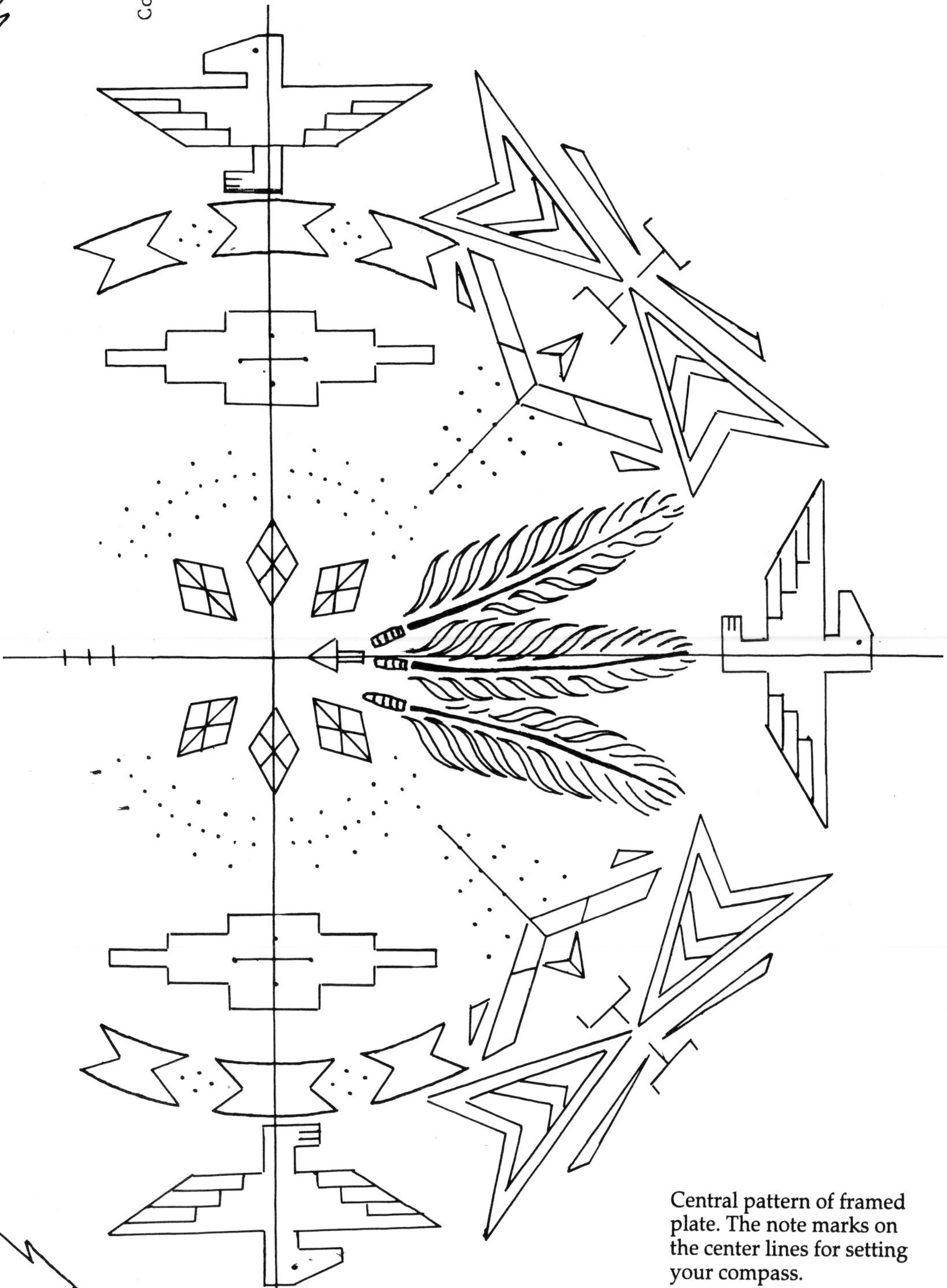

Compass Marks

Central pattern of framed
plate. The note marks on
the center lines for setting
your compass.

9

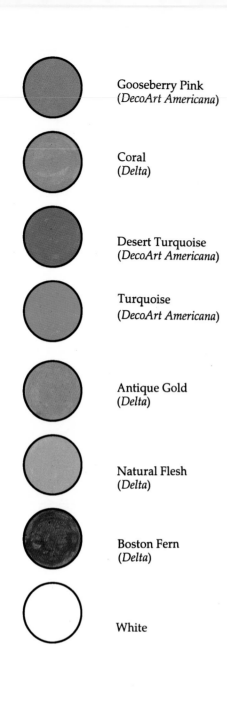

Gooseberry Pink
(*DecoArt Americana*)

Coral
(*Delta*)

Desert Turquoise
(*DecoArt Americana*)

Turquoise
(*DecoArt Americana*)

Antique Gold
(*Delta*)

Natural Flesh
(*Delta*)

Boston Fern
(*Delta*)

White

Candle box pattern for the bottom of the side.

Border design. If your border measurements differ from the example, divide the border evenly and space this design evenly.

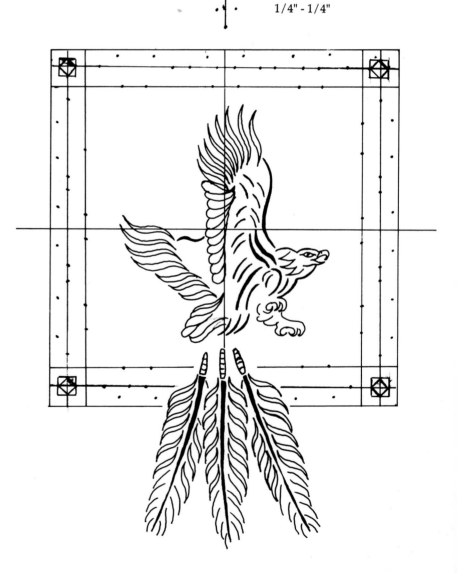

1/4" - 1/4"

Central pattern for the candlebox.

Broom holder pattern.

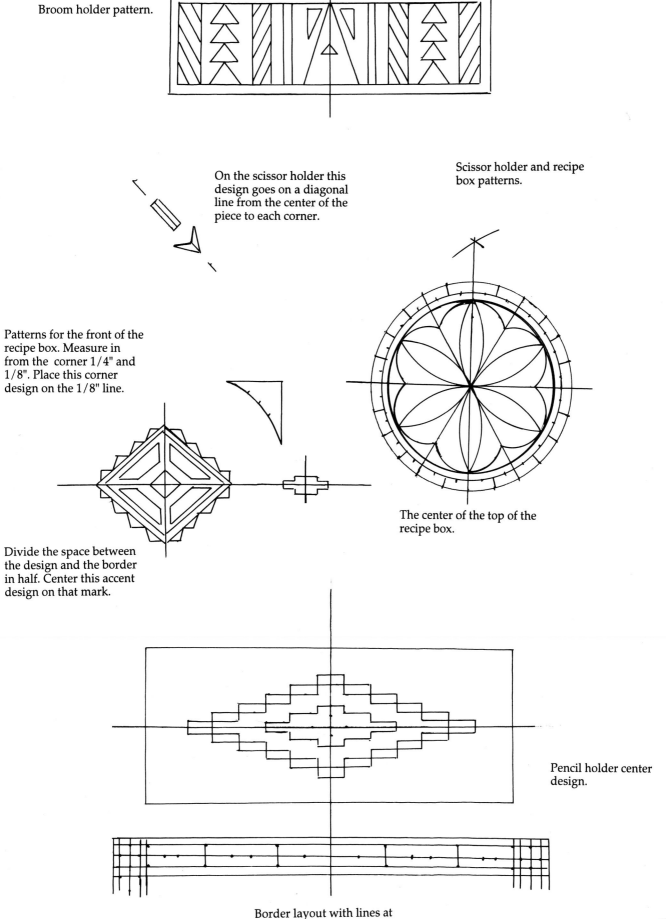

On the scissor holder this design goes on a diagonal line from the center of the piece to each corner.

Scissor holder and recipe box patterns.

Patterns for the front of the recipe box. Measure in from the corner 1/4" and 1/8". Place this corner design on the 1/8" line.

The center of the top of the recipe box.

Divide the space between the design and the border in half. Center this accent design on that mark.

Pencil holder center design.

Border layout with lines at intervals of 2 cm - 4 cm -4 cm- 2 cm from the edge.

Laying Out The Plate

Find the center of the plate, using a compass.

Mark the diameter at equal distances from the center.

Draw a diameter with the grain.

Widen the compass and with the point in the marks you just made, scribe arcs above and below the diameter.

Connect the cross marks through the center to create a line perpendicular to the diameter.

Erase the marks leaving only the diameter and the perpendicular line. Lay the pattern on the plate using the cross hairs as guides. Tape one side down and place a piece of transfer paper between the pattern and the plate. Mark the compass points and the other patterns.

The dots are the points of the geometrical pattern. They will be connected when the pattern is removed.

Draw arcs through the dots that are near the center of the plate. I gave compass marks on the pattern. You can make adjustments to the dots so they are on the lines, or you can just eyeball it.

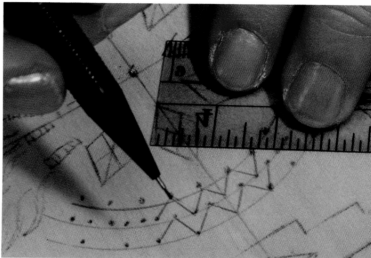

Start drawing the angles from the center line out. When the dots don't fall right on the line, carry the triangles to the line, not to the dots.

Draw a line at each end of the patterns to finish them off.

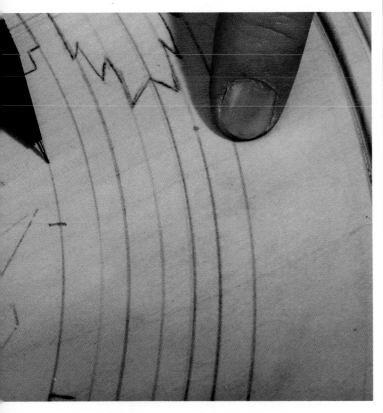

You need seven circles 1/4" apart for the outside decoration of your plate. Where these fall depends on the diameter of the plate you are using. Decide where you want the pattern and draw the circles. The circles can be divided five and two with the two being closest to the center pattern, and any space you want between the two and the five.

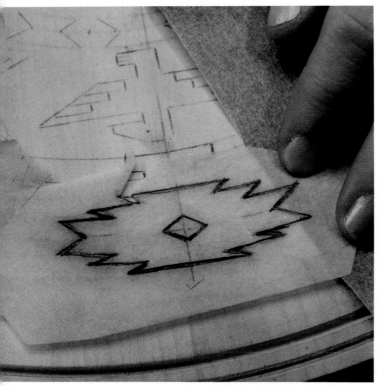

Line this pattern on the outside circle centering it on the four perpendicular lines you drew earlier for layout.

There is a line in the pattern that runs through the triangles and divides the quadrants in half. Extend this line out through the seven circles.

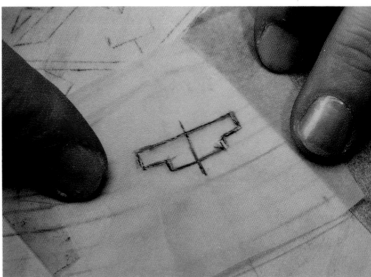

Center this pattern on that line, and align it with the inner-most of the seven circles. Repeat this pattern at each of the four new lines and at each perpendicular line, a total of eight.

Find the center between these patterns.

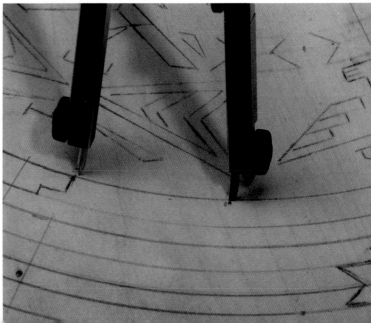

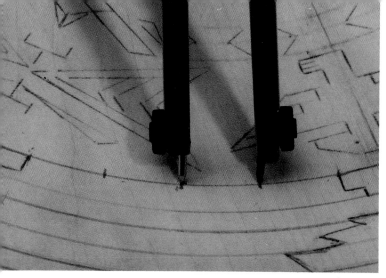

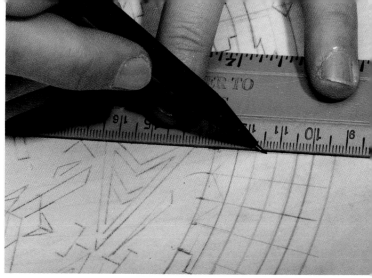

Then find the centers of each of those segments, quartering the original arc.

and draw lines out through the circles.

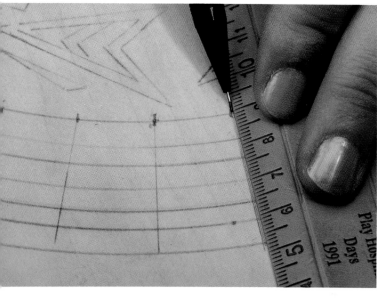

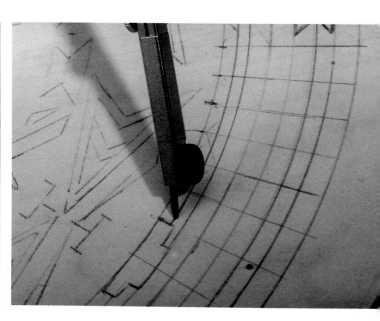

Align a straightedge with the center of the plate and draw lines through these points radiating out through the seven circles.

Draw a circle midway between the first two (innermost) circles.

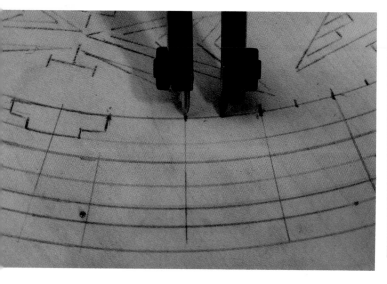

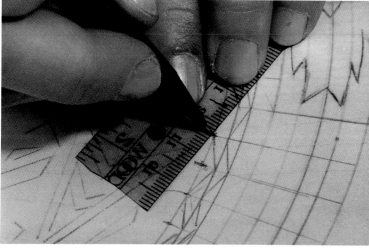

Divide the segments one more time...

Draw parallel diagonals in the inner circles to create a chevron design.

The border arrow design on the outer five circles works out from the pattern that aligns with the feathers in the center. Begin at the first radius on each side of that pattern and draw lines from the center circle to the outside circles, going from radius 1 to radius 4. This diagonal line will cover 3 blocks in length. Draw a straight line down the middle of the arrow.

Draw lines from the points of the arrows to the dots.

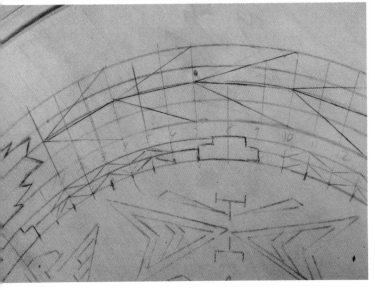

Start the next pattern on the radius where the last one ended and make four arrow shapes. The space between the last arrow and the pattern will be filled with another design element.

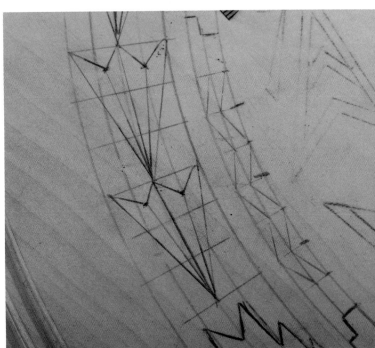

Draw lines from the bottom corners and center to the dots.

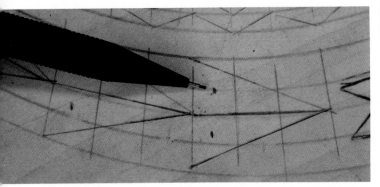

Mark the center between each triangle in the arrow, about 1/4" from the back of the arrowhead. The bottom mark will fall on a line, but the top mark will be slightly inside the line.

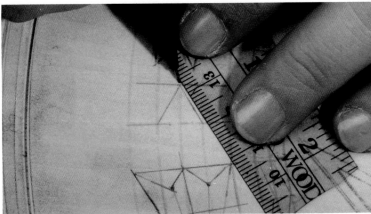

To end the pattern after the last arrow head in the quadrant, draw diagonals from the center circle to the middle circles, one block back.

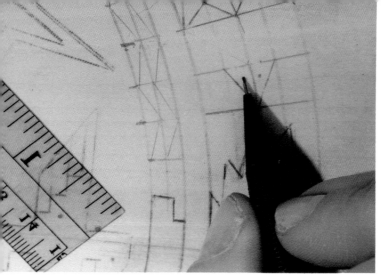

Make a mark in the middle of these small triangles about 1/8" from the line...

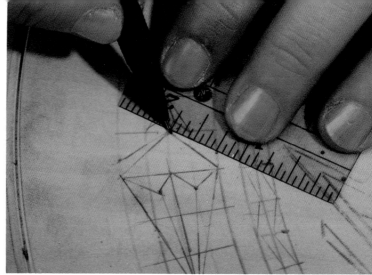

On the outside circles mark a point 1/4" from the corners of the large triangle and connect it to the center point of the small triangle.

and draw lines from the points.

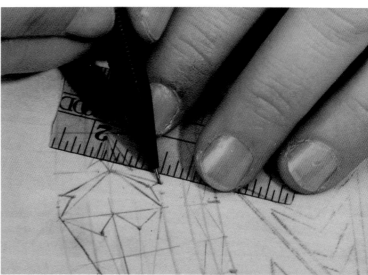

Bisect this triangle with a dot about 1/8" in and connect to the point.

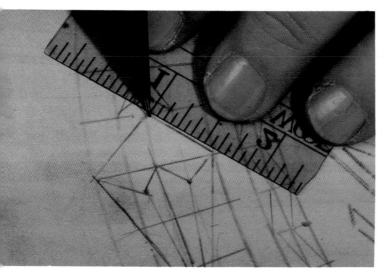

From the center of the small triangle draw back to the corners of the arrowhead pattern.

Connect the dot to the ends of the triangle.

The small diamonds near the center are saved until last, in case I need to use my compass later. The larger center diamonds are essentially a series of triangles. With the knife in Position 1, cut with the grain first...

and the third. The triangle should pop out.

the second cut...

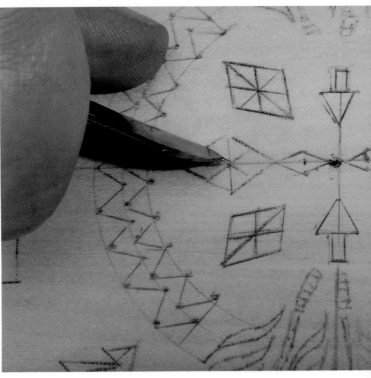

Move to the adjoining triangle and repeat the steps. One cut from the center along the side of the previous triangle...

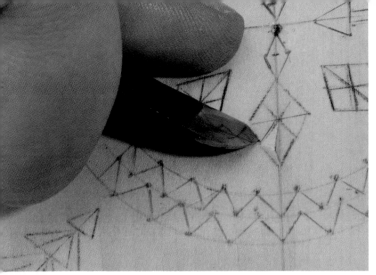

the second cut...

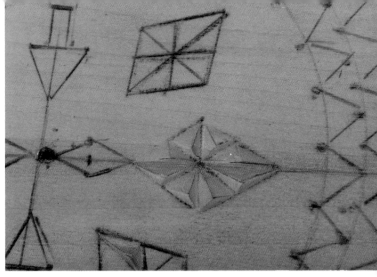

The result.

and the third.

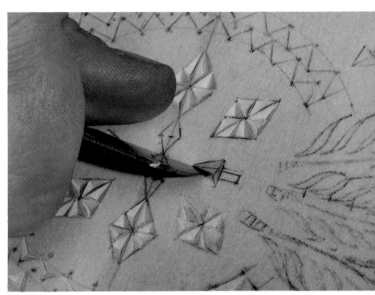

The point of the arrow is three cuts.

Continue around the diamond in the same way until you come back to the original triangle.

The tail takes a stop cut at the end...

and cuts along the edges.

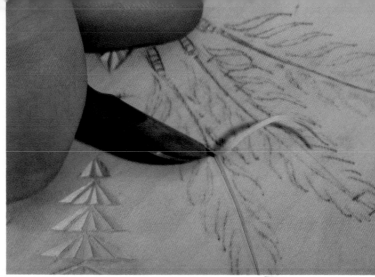

Come back down the other side of the spine, starting with the knife straight and gradually laying it over slightly.

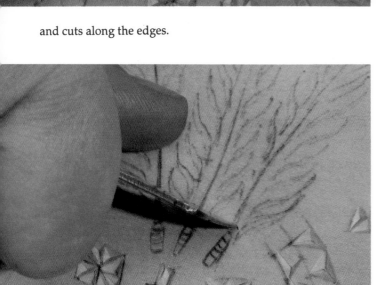

At the bottom of the spines of the feathers make stop cuts.

Cut the vanes of the feather with two strokes, cutting out...

From the stop cut the length of the spine with the knife slightly laid over at the beginning and straight at the end.

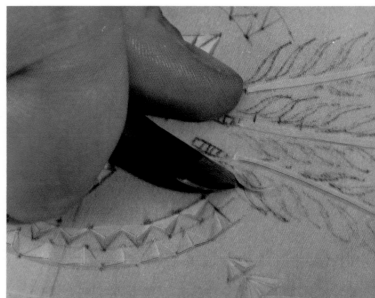

turning the work and cutting back.

As you approach the tip of the feather, the vanes get straighter.

Cut a stop at both ends of the tips of the feathers.

With two cuts cut lines along the outside edges of the tips.

Trim back to the stops at each end...

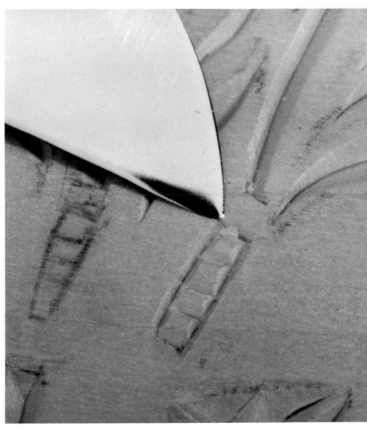

and incise the lines for this effect.

The feathers done.

the second in Position 2...

and the third in Position 1.

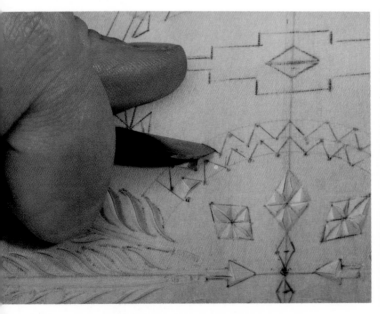

The jagged border is created by removing triangles. This is done with three cuts. The first in Position 1...

The result.

The chevron of triangles is carved as a series of triangles, all done in Position 1. Each triangle has three cuts. One...

Move to the adjacent triangle and repeat the process.

two...

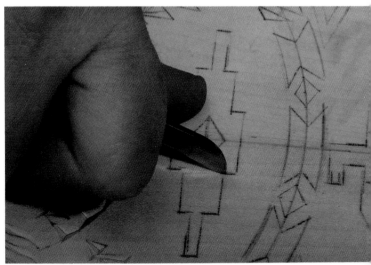

On the next pattern make stops at the ends of all the straight lines. Because two lines come into each step that means two stops in each step, or 20 in the pattern.

three.

Cut along the lines with the knife slightly laid over.

Come back in the other direction to incise the line.

On the other triangle come down the adjoining side with the knife in Position 1.

Go back and incise the steps.

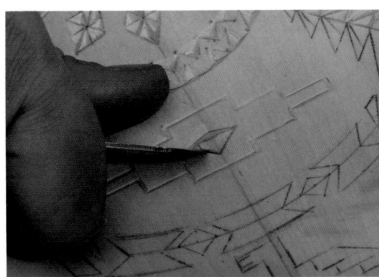

Turn the board and cut the second side, also in Position 1.

The diamond in the middle is two adjoining triangles. Cut one with three cuts, Position 1, Position 2, Position 1.

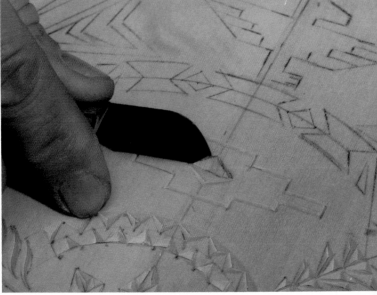

The third side is cut in Position 2.

Make stops at the ends of the long lines of this chevron...

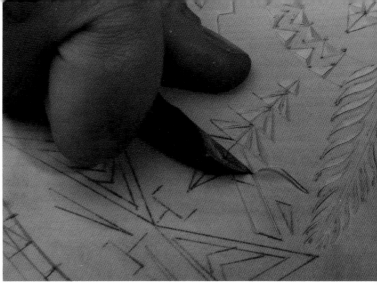

Incise the long lines.

and where the two sides meet here...

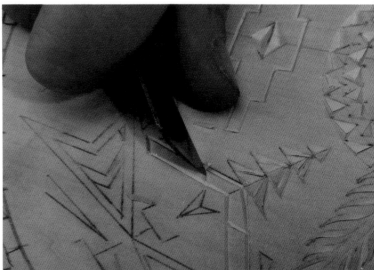

Incise the ends and these lines across the arm.

and here.

These small triangles are done in Position 1.

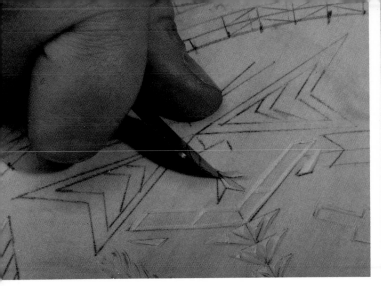

The first of these adjacent triangles is done in three cuts, Position 1, Position 2, Position 1.

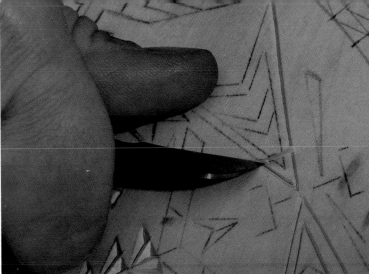

Incise the outlines of the outer and inner triangles. When the two lines meet at the point, you want to cut the inside of the line first to ensure that they meet properly.

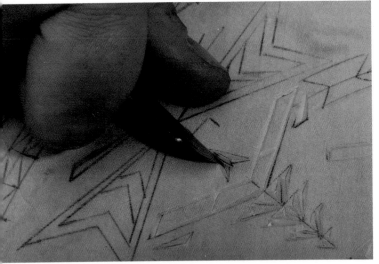

The other is also done in three cuts, beginning with the shared side, but all are done in Position 1.

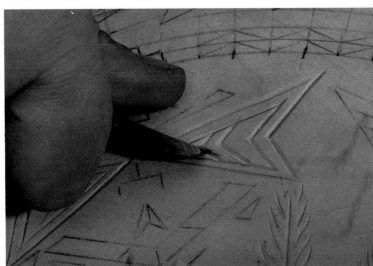

Incise the chevrons.

Make stops at the end of any long line of this pattern.

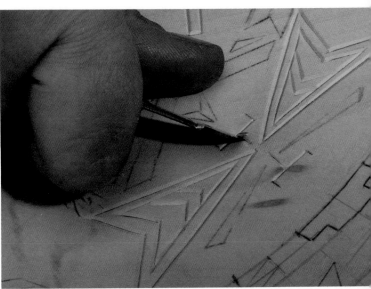

Incise the lines of the decorative pattern.

26

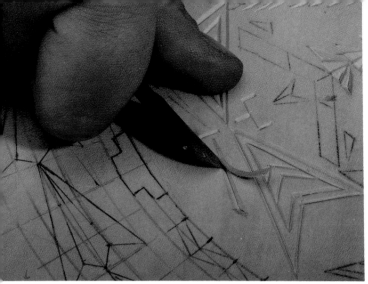

Cut the elongated triangles in three cuts.

Incise the top and bottom lines.

The ribbon beneath the thunderbird has stop cuts at the ends of all the long lines...

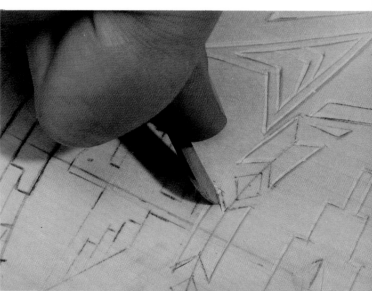

On the ends make the inside cuts first, cutting back into the point.

and at the inner points.

Come back and cut out the line from the outside.

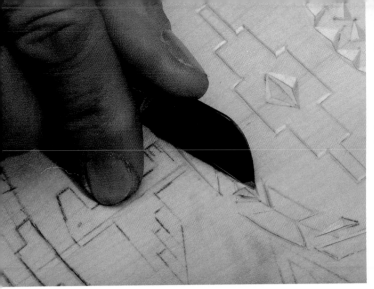

The diamond is done as before.

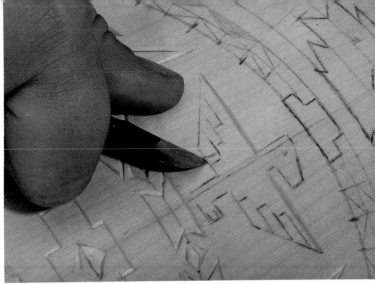

Incise the lines.

Make diagonal stop cuts at the ends of the wings.

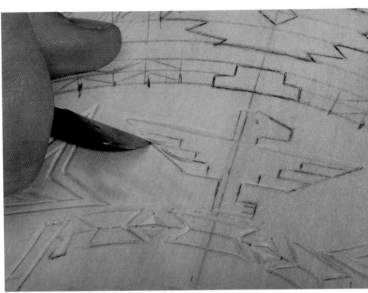

On the diagonals, make the first cut on the inside of the line.

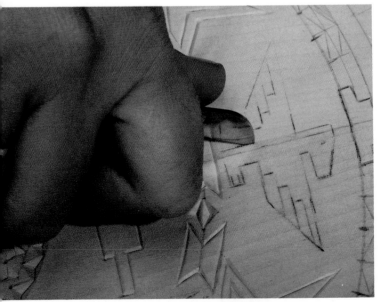

Make stop cuts at the ends of the rest of the straight lines.

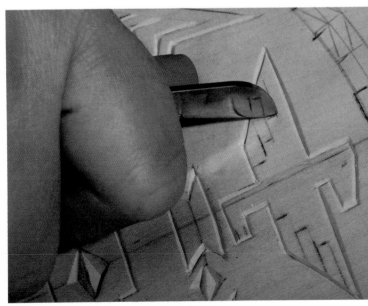

Make stops at the end of the feather lines.

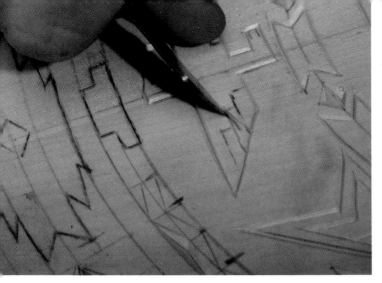

Incise the lines of the feathers.

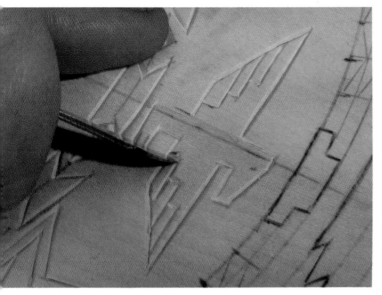

Finish with the end lines.

With a nail punch, poke the eye.

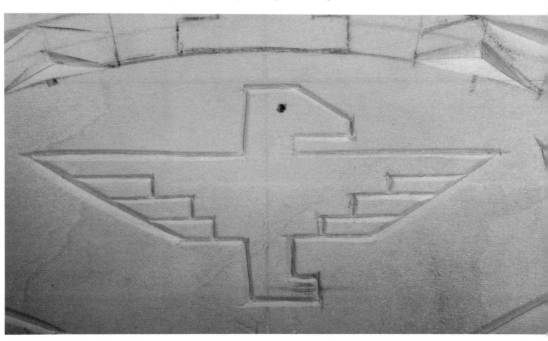

The result.

This small step is done just like the double step pattern we did earlier.

and perpendicular to the long lines at the other angles. Also make a stop at every outside point.

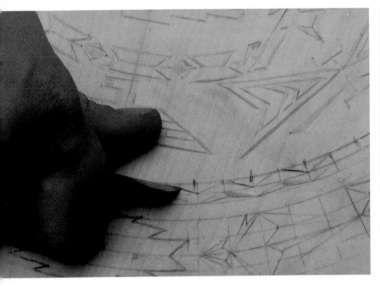

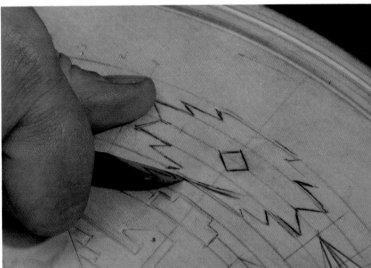

This zig-zag pattern is like the one around the center of the plate.

Incise the long lines.

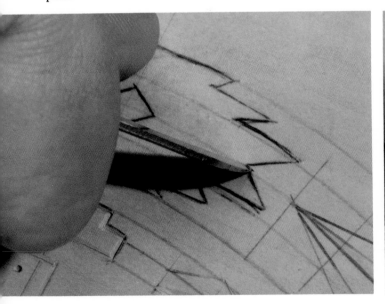

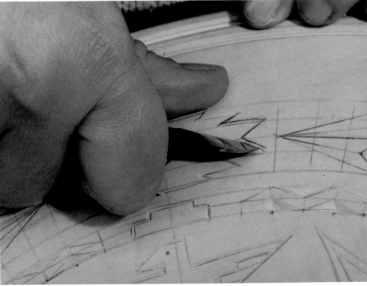

Cut a stop this way at the ends of this pattern...

At the points the first cut is away from the inside of the point.

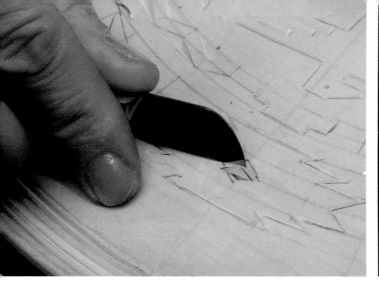

Do the adjoining triangles of the middle as you did before to form the diamond.

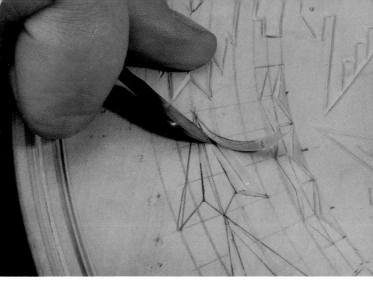

Come up the other side.

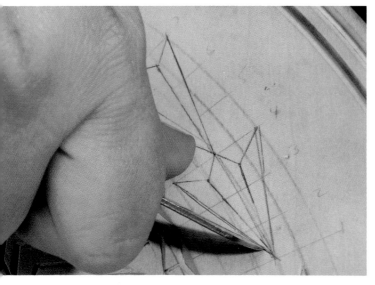

The adjacent elongated triangles begin with a cut in Position 1 down the long side. Start with the blade straight up and end with it laid over.

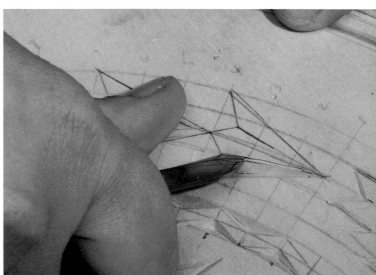

The adjacent triangle is carved in Position 1, with three cuts. One...

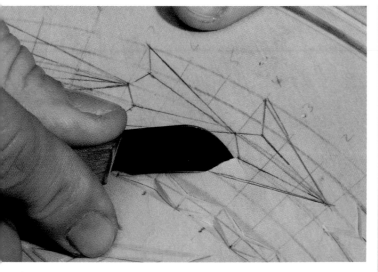

For the second cut it seems natural to use Position 2 and cut the end.

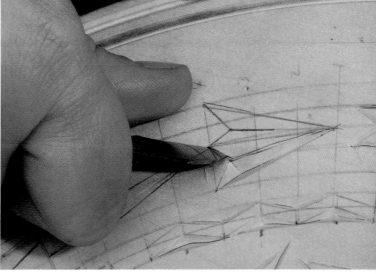

two...

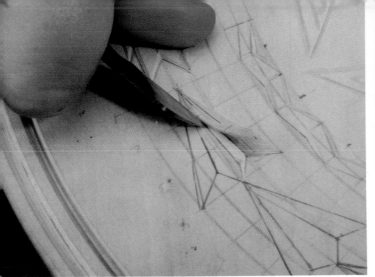

three.

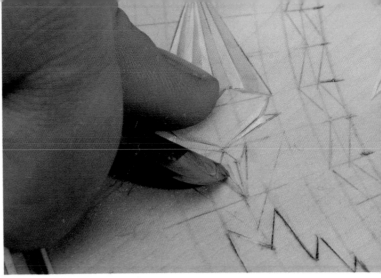

This element, too, is done in the same way, but because it is smaller it requires a lighter touch and more finesse.

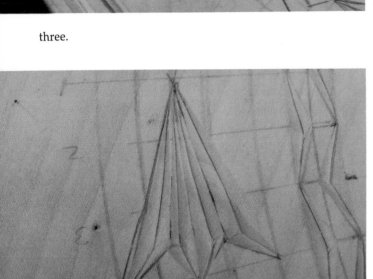

The third triangle is done like the first and the fourth is like the second for this result.

Cut the diamonds in the center.

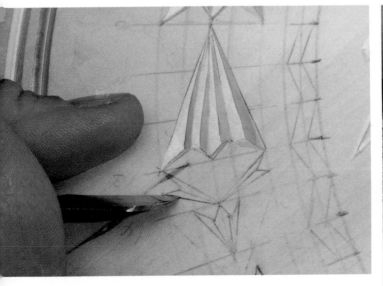

These adjoining triangles are like the first two cuts of the element we just completed.

Draw small lines from diamond to diamond.

Make stab cuts in these lines, going straight in...   and pulling the blade down.

The finished plate.

The Candle Box

On the front of the candle box, make three 1/4" marks from the edge.

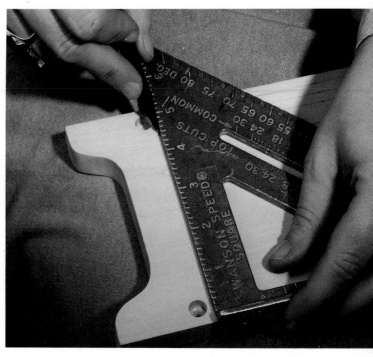

Measure down an inch from the center part of the top edge and come across using a square.

Measure 2" from the bottom.

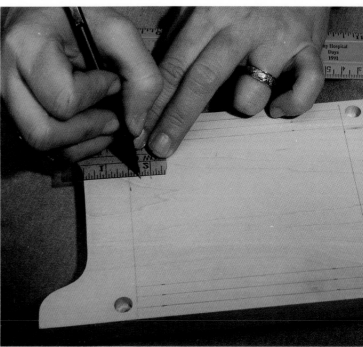

Measure down two 1/4" marks from the top line and draw lines across with a ruler.

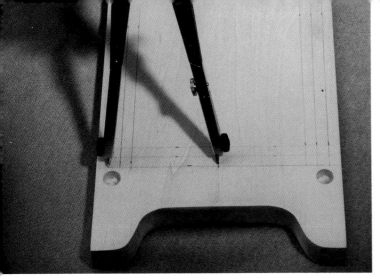

Find and mark the centers of all four sides.

Where the lines cross in the top corners measure from the center out 1/8" on all four lines.

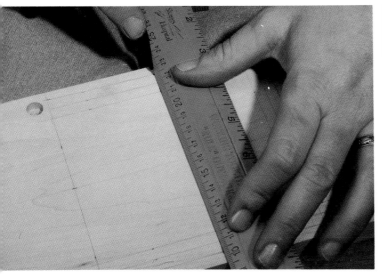

Draw the perpendicular lines through the centers.

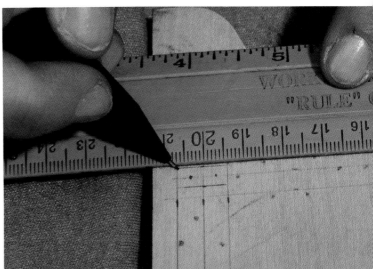

Draw lines through the 1/8" marks.

Align the pattern with the crossed perpendiculars, tape it in place, lay tracing paper between the pattern and the wood and draw it.

The same is done at the bottom, but first you have to establish the quarter inch marks.

When the bottom is marked out you can complete the boxes in the four corners.

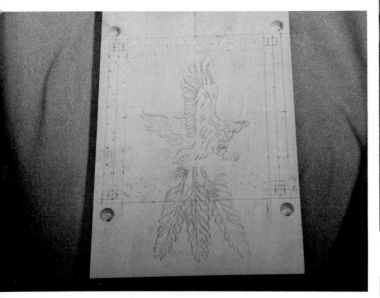

The result is a box in each corner which then has a diamond drawn within it.

Connect dots to form the pattern around large box.

This is how the pattern will look when it is complete.

On the sides of the candle box measure in 1/4" from the long edges and the bottom, and draw lines.

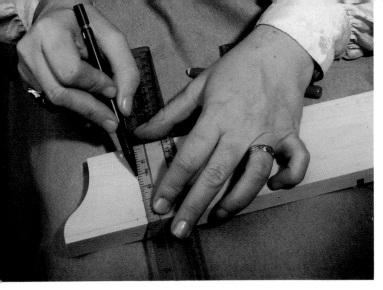

Measure up from the bottom 3", 10 1/2" and 10 3/4" and draw lines.

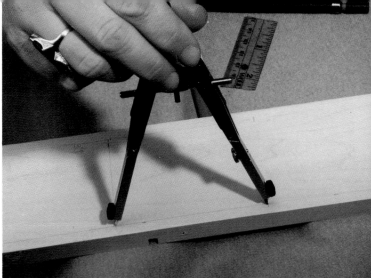

Find the center between the 3" and the 10 1/2" lines (the two inside lines)...

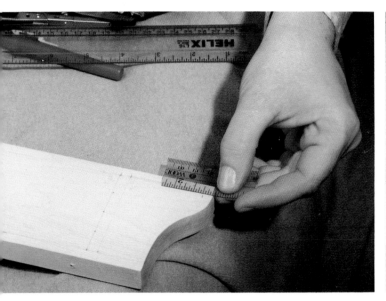

Measure and mark 1/4" from the top corner of the side.

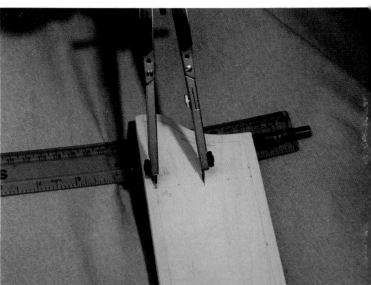

and the centers of the top and bottom.

Set your compass to this mark and use it to copy the curve of the top. The decorative line in the center of this edge is done in the same way, but is another eighth inch in.

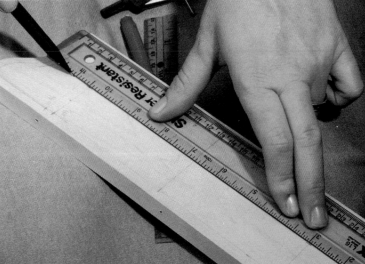

Draw the long center line from the very top of the piece to the very bottom.

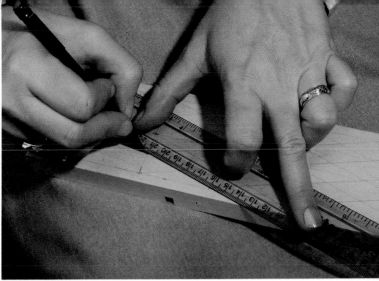

The rectangle of the grid area needs to be divided again. Divide the long side...

and the other to create diamonds.

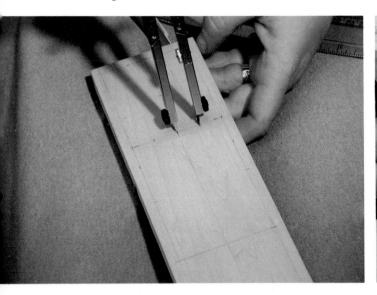

and the short side.

Align the ruler at the crossing points of the diamonds and mark the ends and sides. This will bisect the lines again, and allow you to double the number of diamonds.

Draw diagonals one way...

Connect them as you did before.

Beginning where a diamond point touches the bottom line draw lines through the diamonds to the top.

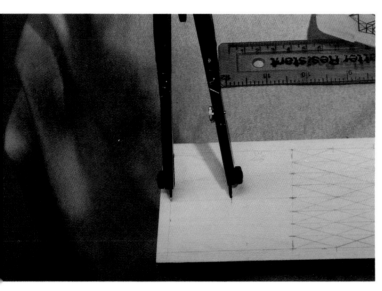

Find the centers of the bottom and the top sections and mark them.

To make the diamond at the top measure 1/4" from center above and below the axis and 1/8" inch to each side and connect the dots.

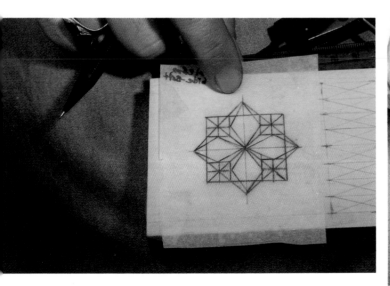

Lay the fancy diamond pattern at the bottom and trace it. Use a straight edge to keep the lines crisp and accurate.

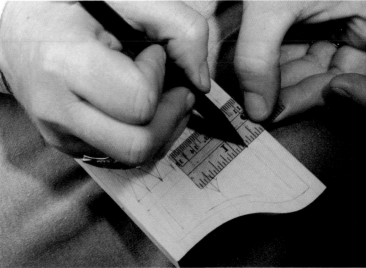

Two accent lines come down the sides of the top.

Carving The Candle Box

Many of the elements of the candle box are the same as those we earlier did in the plate. The feathers are nearly identical to those on the plate.

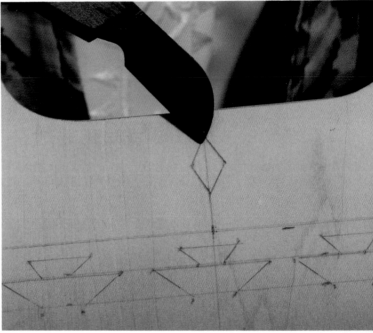

The diamond...

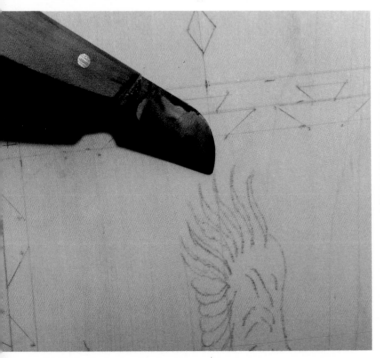

The feathers of the eagle are the same s-curve as the large feathers.

and the border were all used on the plate.

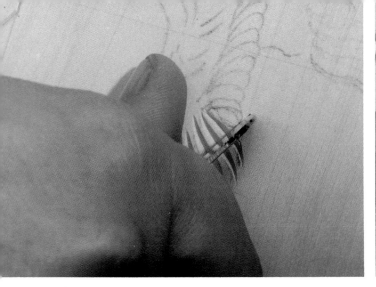

We begin the eagle by carving the s-curve feathers at the tip of the wing. At the back of the wing we move to a rounded feather, making this transition point critical. Start here...

and curve up a little at the end...

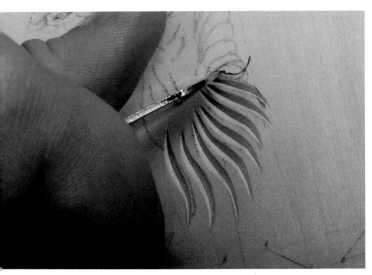

and with very little pressure cut around to here and stop.

for this result. The feather is much rounder than the s-feathers, but still has a hint of the curve.

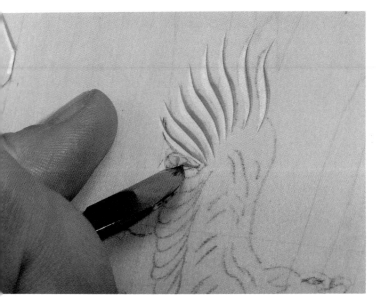

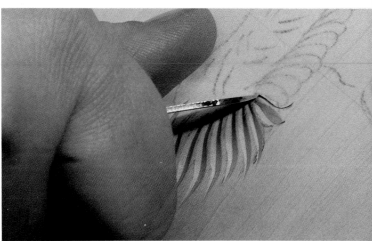

Cut back here...

On these rounded feathers you may not be able to follow the pattern exactly, the tendency being to go larger than what   is drawn. Just be consistent from one feather to the next. Cut from the end to the wing with the s-curved cut, digging the knife in at the rounded end.

41

Come back with a round cut to finish the feather.

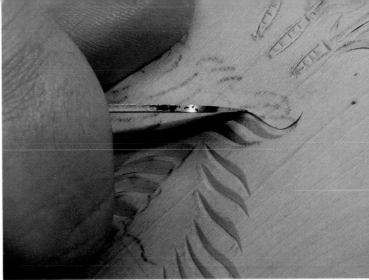

The next tail feather is transitional. The top cut follows the line of the s-curve above.

The result.

The bottom cut starts straight and rounds up at the end...

The other wing and the top two tail feathers are simple s-curves, thought the tail feathers are almost adjoining.

for this result.

The top edge of the next feather follows the line of the one above.

One more feather finishes the tail.

The bottom edge flares out before turning back.

An s-cut forms the front edge of the back wing.

The result.

The front edge of the forward wing is a long s-curve. The knife starts straight, is laid over dramatically in the middle, and ends in straight. This gives a dynamic effect.

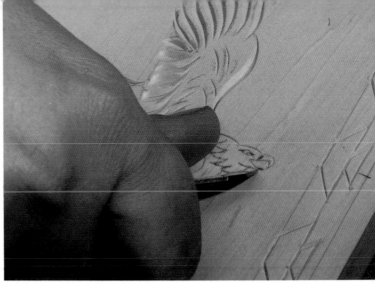

Lines on the top of the neck and head take us to the beak. The top of the beak is cut in one line, with no pressure in the hand, so the knife cuts just the top fibers of the wood. Go to the point of the beak.

the lower beak...

Go back to complete the line of the top of the beak.

the head feathers...

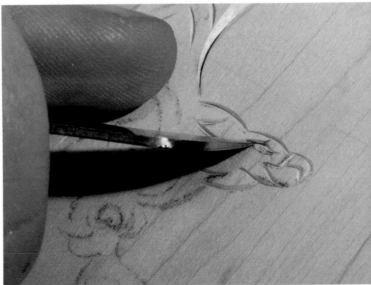

Use the same light touch on the underside of the upper beak...

and the eye. The eye is an even more delicate cut. The top is an s-curve.

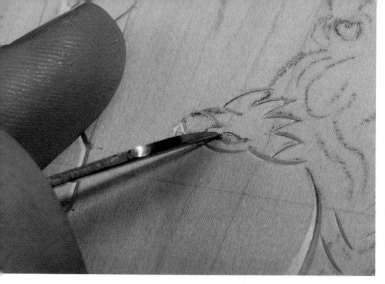

The bottom is rounder.

Do the bottom leg and claw in the same way.

Use light pressure as you go around the round line of the shoulder. The grain wants to carry the knife if you apply too much pressure.

Poke the eye and the nostril of the beak with a nail set, and the eagle is finished.

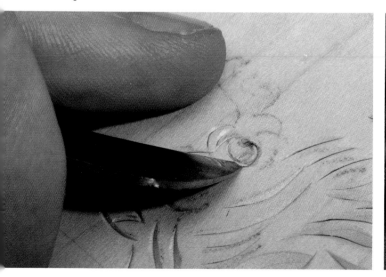

Cut the lines of the talons. The front of the back talon joins with the back of the second front talon.

Cut the four sides of the corner design.

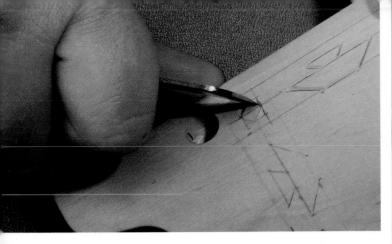

Cut the edges of the center diamond, to pop out triangles at the corners.

Two triangles are cut inside the diamond. Starting across the center cut one triangle using Positions 1-2-1. The other triangle is cut in Positions 1-1-2.

This is the result.

Cut the straight lines, making the first cut away from the carved patterns.

Make stop cuts at the feathers where the lines end.

The front of the candle box completed.

When you lay the grid pattern on the side, you end up with diamonds with lines running through them from top to bottom. These are the diamonds that will be carved. Begin at one end of the pattern and work to the other.

The third is along the shared side and is in Position 1. The knife starts straight, lays over in the middle, and ends straight.

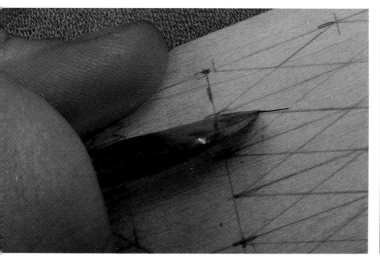

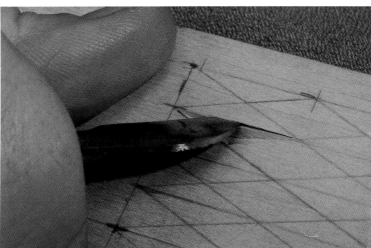

The diamonds require six cuts. The first is in Position 1 beginning with the knife laid over and moving to straight up and down.

The fourth cut is along the other side of the shared edge and is done in the same way.

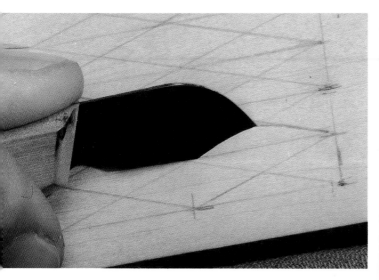

The second is in Position 2 and also moves from having the knife laid over to having it straight.

The next cut is in Position 1 as well...

and the last cut is in Position 2.

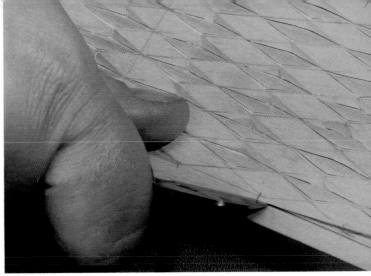

and cut the lines.

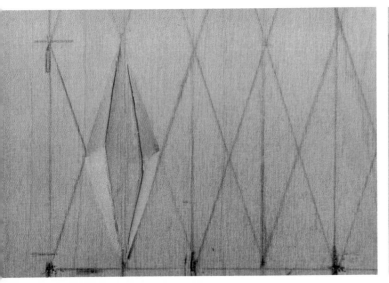

The result. This pattern is repeated in every diamond with a line. When you are comfortable you can do the same cut across all the diamonds in a row, before turning the board. This saves time and energy.

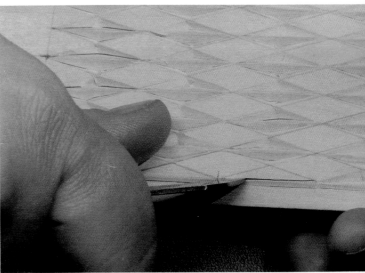

The half diamonds at the edges need to have the long side cut first to avoid cutting into the border line.

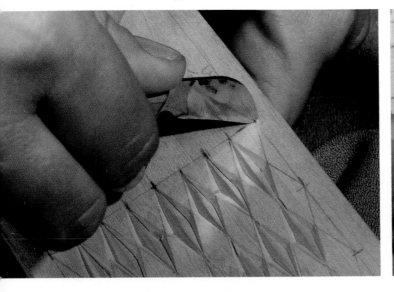

Cut stops at the ends of the edge lines...

Cut the other two sides as you did before.

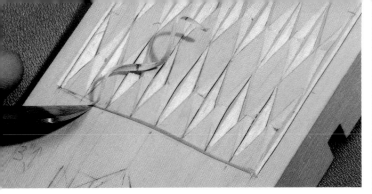

Cut the borderlines at the ends, staying away from the points of the triangle.

Cut three.

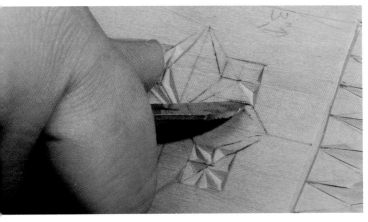

The corners of this element are a series of adjacent triangles within a square and are done in the same way as the elements in the center of the plate.

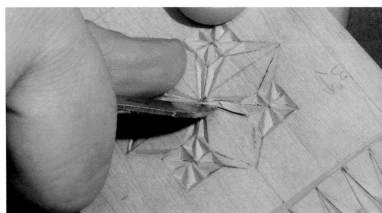

Repeat on the other side.

Cut the line at the top and the side is complete.

Between the diamonds of this element are two adjacent elongated triangles. Make the first cut toward the corner, being careful not to cut into the square.

Cut two.

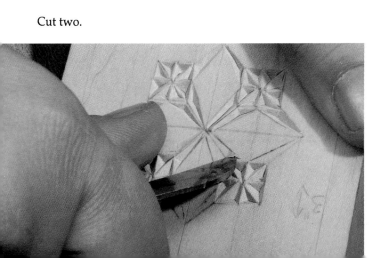

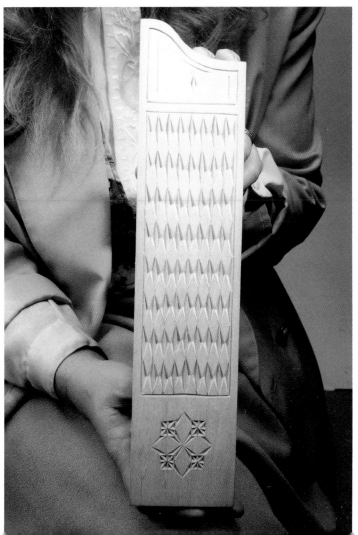

The Octagonal Border

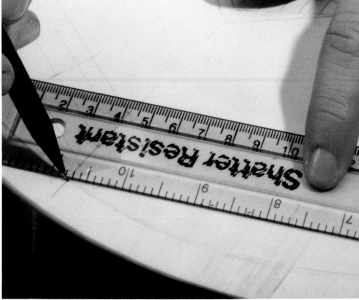

The other plate can be carved using techniques used earlier in the book. The only really new problem is laying out the octagonal border. This happens after you trace the pattern in the center of the plate. Draw a circle 3/4" in from the edge and extend the four perpendicular lines out to the center.

Draw a line from the perpendicular line to the midpoint mark.

Divide the arcs between the perpendicular in half.

Repeat around the plate.

Draw a line from the center to the midpoint in the arc. From the outside circle measure and mark points 1/4", 3/8", 3/8", and 1/4" apart.

then divide and mark again.

Connect the marks on each line to the next.

Draw perpendicular lines through the marks, over all five lines. The clear ruler allows me to use the inch markers as a kind of miniature square, aligning them with my lines and drawing along the straightedge.

Divide these segments in half and mark...

Draw diagonals from corner to corner of each section in the three inner lines.

Where the diamonds meet, draw another perpendicular, carrying it through all five lines.

Align the ruler to draw smaller diamonds between the valleys of the larger diamonds.

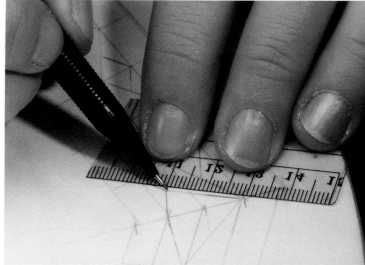

Finally draw a line from this point to the end of the small diamond.

The last small diamonds before the radius use the center line for alignment.

Draw diagonals across the sections of the outside lines. This will alternate direction from section to section, as you can see from the finished plate.

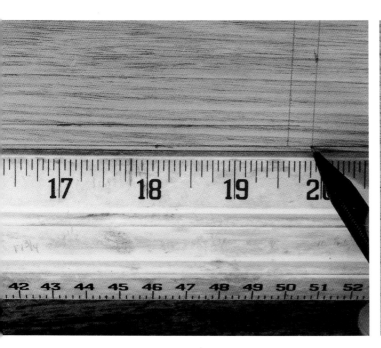

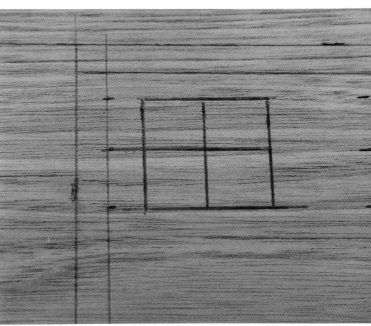

The Thunderbird plaque involves carving techniques that you have already learned. The layout is somewhat complicated, however. As always, begin by laying the horizontal and vertical midlines. Then measure in from the edges 1" and 1/4" and draw lines around the border.

Draw lines to make this four-part box.

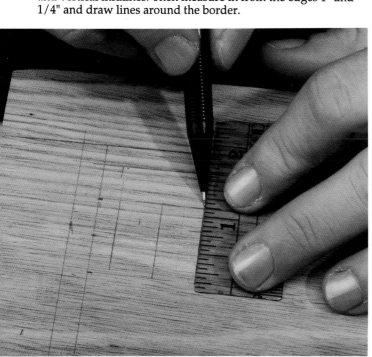

From the outside line of the corner measure in from each side and make 3 marks at 1/2" intervals.

Align the pattern with the inside of the 1/4" border and 1/8" from the corner box. Tape it and trace it.

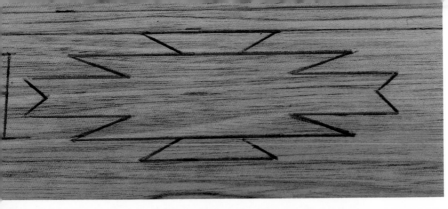

The pattern.

The second pattern is centered on the board and the third is centered between the first and second. Use a compass to find the correct position.

Use the crosslines to lay the thunderbird pattern in place. Use a straightedge when doing these lines.

Between each of the border patterns find center and draw the triangles back to back, with 1/4" between. Continue the process all around the border. On the short sides the middle pattern is centered, and the end patterns begin 1/8" from the corner box, as they did on the long side.

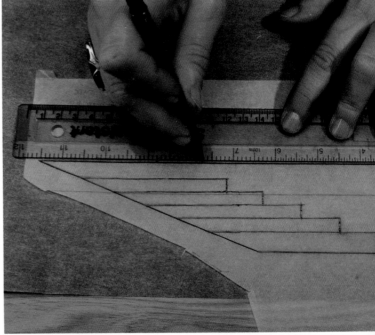

When one side is drawn turn the pattern over and align it, and trace just the wing portion.

54

The pattern above the thunderbird's wings start 5 3/4" below the top edge and is centered between the small triangles that are between the first and second border patterns.

From that line draw three others at 1/4" intervals.

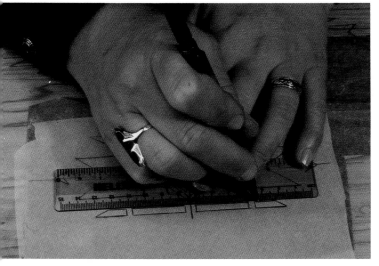

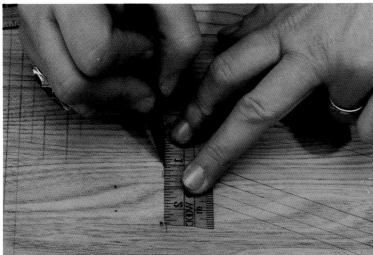

Tape and draw the pattern.

Come in from the edge 4 1/2" and draw an end line parallel to the edge of the plaque.

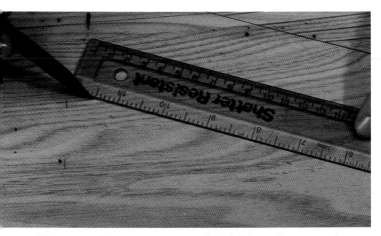

The center chevrons are centered 4 1/2" from the top on the center line. The stripes below the wings are parallel to the underside of the wing. The way I found the line was by simply laying my ruler along the edge and marking, then repeating the process. This second line is the top line of the striped pattern.

Measure 5 1/2" or whatever you like down the top and the bottom line of the stripe and join the points for the other end.

Returning to the corners, draw diagonals in each direction through the four-part box.

Measure 1/16" on each side of the diagonals...

and draw lines. The space between these lines will be left uncut.

Candle Box

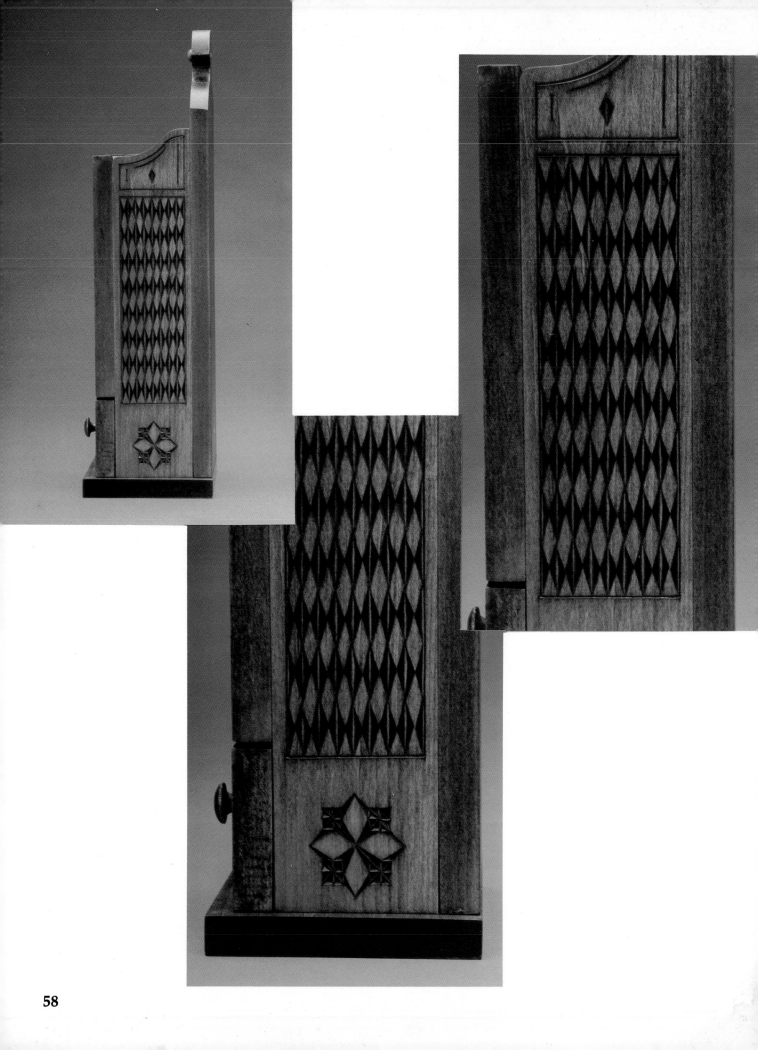

Plate

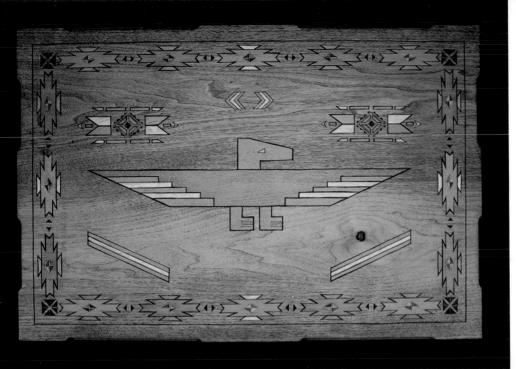

Thunderbird
Plaque

Recipe Box

Kitchen Utensil or
Dried Flower Box

Broom Holder

Framed Plate

Scissor Holder

Pencil Holder

64